People Look Like Ants from Up Here

Abhishek Sikhwal

PublishAmerica
Baltimore

© 2005 by Abhishek Sikhwal.

All rights reserved. No part of this book may be reproduced, stored in a retrieval system or transmitted in any form or by any means without the prior written permission of the publishers, except by a reviewer who may quote brief passages in a review to be printed in a newspaper, magazine or journal.

First printing

ISBN: 1-4137-6064-3
PUBLISHED BY PUBLISHAMERICA, LLLP
www.publishamerica.com
Baltimore

Printed in the United States of America

This one is for Yossarin... my fifty-five missions

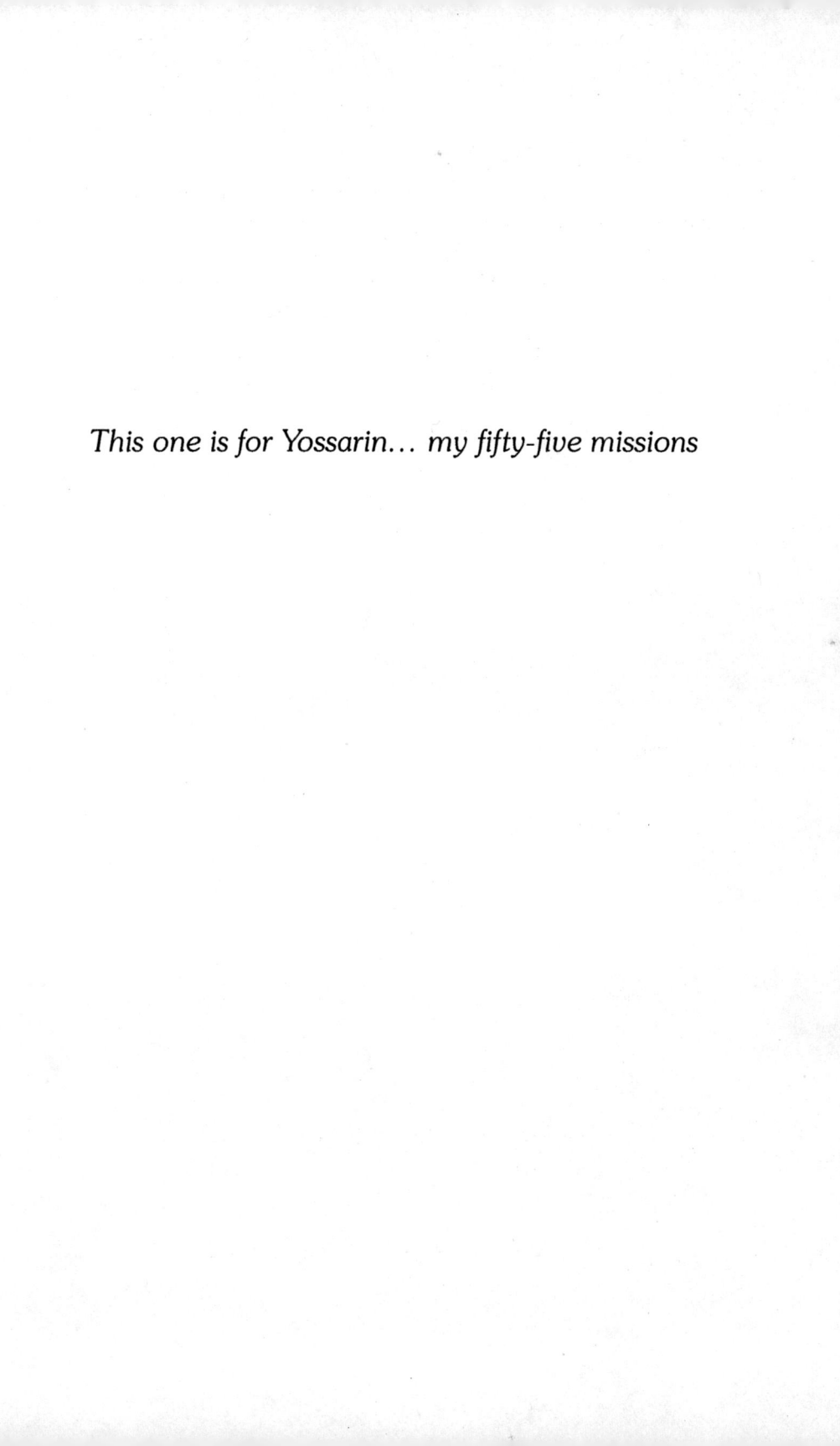

People Look Like Ants from Up Here

And so a soldier of verve marched into a town,
Nothing left in this parish, save an eternal frown.
Bedrooms full of bullets and living rooms with no one living,
The populace all but dead and no one around for grieving.
He was a participant to free this fevered nation, or so he thought,
But now it felt he was just a usual ingredient in an unusual broth.
And as he looked around, something caught his eye:
A shirtless boy standing on a roof, in the heat of July.
Curious by the boy's stance, he stepped aside from the troop,
Carrying his gun all day had made his shoulders droop.
"Boy, get down from there and go home fast!"
"They barraged my house and razed my past."
"Is your father up with you as well?"
"Oh, he is much higher, the courtesy of a shell."
The soldier now red, could conjure up no consolation,
Even the gun in his hands couldn't handle this lost confrontation.
And he wouldn't have spoken but the boy had something to ask:
"Is killing innocent people your daily task?"
"No, we are here to unshackle your nation."
"Look around you, sir, and show me liberation."
"Freedom can't be shown, it lives in the air."
"But flames are easier to see, can't you see them everywhere?"
The soldier started walking with the gun gripped in his hands,
He said, "I'm not the one to blame, son, I just follow commands."
"You came to free me," the boy said, "but don't be surprised if I don't cheer,
Because I stand alone and people look like ants from up here."

Shoes Are Tied, Help Me Decide

One road will take me to sky-scrapers, trains, subways and a desk,
Behind which I need not ask for directions. The neon lights
Are agreeable to look at, but so are snakes, and they both curl up and lapse
In a hiss. Me, a man of loose core
And ears that have a passion for wandering, I may swoon
If all their phone calls and modems and sighs march into my fort.
No mortals here, I'm afraid, just citizens who'll look
Me up and down and often donate
Smiles.

The other will take me to fields where there are no jobs and
Thorns bejewel the path. Folks could be colder than the pawns
On a chess board but chess is a game
I know all too well. Boredom could come like
A chewing in-law who just doesn't know when it's time
To part. But there are chances
That walking a long day, I'll meet some village girl
Whom I could tell a joke only I know and make her
Laugh.

Yes, I, too, think I shouldn't wilt in the city,
I'd rather take my chances with simplicity.

Superstitions

In the kitchen of mystery, the mice gaze
At how humans find a black cat ominous,
An intelligent race choking on an unreal haze,
In the folly of finding someone more poisonous.
And mirrors are mirrors and they must assume
We humans are hideous in thoughts as well,
Feeding absurdity by following fume,
Broken glass rings a bell.
As a human I do believe
Old notions make our tribe a tangled kitten,
Make us unable to soupcon the lush alpines.
And if you don't like what I've written,
Is it because this poem has thirteen lines?

Aftermath

The door is shut and so is my mind
Because they both only open to things left behind,
Today I'm awake and think of the day
When I told you I loved you in the strangest way.

Many years to live concludes my doctor
But the view is too lonely from this helicopter,
You made every day a reason to persevere,
Now you have to come back for the conditions are severe.

The television is stinging and the ads haven't even started,
How can I buy shampoo when I'm so broken-hearted?
The memory remains and it remains for long,
All my rights now only seem wrong.

I need you in my arms and to smell your perfume
My bed is now a desert and my eyes a ridiculous flume,
I need someone around me who doesn't don a frown,
'Cause with you gone... I'm the loneliest boy in town.

A Ticking Planet

Me waking up every morning in bed,
Awash with realms which some are yet to wed,
Knotted with a craving to one day spin the lair,
End all the comic villainy with which I have to bear.

Me and you can sit down and talk,
Of bad yesterdays and a tomorrow made of chalk,
Naked knives are arranged in the bouquet of power
Every blonde hope appears a brunette from this tower,
You and I can have better chows to devour.

Nudged into alleys where once people sang
Of good tomorrows… until shushed by a fat and little bang,
Today we must pick up a phone that never rang.

Where we'll meet again, I'm not too sure,
Alone stands he who can't see amusement in endure,
Reasons are diseases but battles never a cure.

A Talk with Myself on the Last Day

"Now you're a fine fellow
Like any other with your flamed eyes,
And yet so out of the lot.
Childhood saw you staggering with nursery rhymes
And at thirty-seven the frost still survives
As you become another hungry lion
In this zoo.
The house like an unfed dog waits for
You to part the doors,
For there is nowhere to go but away
And nothing to do but
Come back.
This house used to be a home,
But not since you started
Smelling the cigarettes your father
Used to smoke and you can *taste* your mother's cookies.
Only a minuscule problem,
You see,
They are dead.
Gone to a 'better place,' the courtesy of faulty brakes and a
Bottle of wine.
A place where three-piece matching leather suitcases stand out
Like baseball in Italian.

Yet here you are with a bottle in palm,
Kissing it like it was a birch.
And I know how you want to end it all;
I can sniff a gun.
Beware, for when left to our own devices
We are all but human.
Today is an important day,
For the rest of your life could be niggling.
All you need is a novel sleep,
Not a slumber without an awakening.
An office of bliss, life certainly isn't,
Nor is death,
So let your heart interrupt the mind.
In the market of flattery only
Fools buy.
And in the market of verve only
Fools die.
So sleep like there is there no tomorrow
But remember there is.
And awake like there was no yesterday
'Cause there never is.
And when you face a new man in the mirror,
One not stabbed by the past, look him
In the eye, and remind *him* to pay the
Electricity bill.
Today was the last day."

Behind My Sunglasses

Behind my sunglasses
The green grass is not green,
I'm someone else and I'm not mean,
I can see you but can't be seen.

Behind my sunglasses
The brawny sun is not so commanding,
Wicked women are not so demanding,
The roads lie straight and not winding.

Behind my sunglasses
People are not an unsolved puzzle,
I can easily stare into a laden muzzle,
My eyes find an atoll where they can nuzzle.

Behind my sunglasses
You are someone not so bad,
The wind blows but makes me glad,
The color swallows all that's sad.

Behind my sunglasses
I'm a step ahead of the masses,
I know everyone who before me passes,
Unless, of course, if they are behind sunglasses.

A Small Town

Take a walk in my heart, darling,
There are things here you haven't seen,
Here is each of your coming destinations furling,
And also all the places you've been.

I have built this metropolis with you in mind,
And hence there is an absence of traffic,
In here lie the treasures you are yet to find,
If a little walking doesn't make you sick.

I had no marble within so couldn't fabricate a pastel structure,
No fountains as well for they're prodigal to the last degree,
But don't you start packing your bags for departure,
'Cause there is an abundance of you and just enough of me.

No ticking bombs and no pricking women, I don't lie
I can wrap up a sunset or two if you stay long,
There are beaches and gardens where we could lie
And listen to nothing but your favorite song.

I know it's not a tourist attraction,
It's not Agra, Rome or Pisa
But you can visit whenever on vacation,
For in my heart you don't require a visa.

Communication

In the times of now
We have machines with memories of a trillion bytes,
They have the telephone altered a bit and now
Available with fifty-six or more connections and
Can be connected to your computer for
Cheaper call rates to Alaska.
They have the electronic mail which makes
Constant messaging for crying pockets a possibility,
And the chat system for meeting a stranger in a stranger place,
An unseen darkness and yet a bliss
For bored housewives and girls sixteen.
And who can overlook the courier's pace delivering love
From Tanzania to Sri Lanka in a
Matter of hours?
Interactive television, much like a science-fiction dream,
You would talk to it like you would to a
Man.
Fax-machines for transfer of modern-art from
One point to another... without a point.

The world is but a stage and we all play our parts,
Some of us place an Inca mummy beside and
Videoconference with unfastened women.
And companies say that humans are
In a communication arena,
As never before; faster-better-cheaper
(mobile phones for twenty dollars!)
Truly as never before.
But what my aloof mind questions is that
With harmony and love at our fingertips, and
With distance no wall,
How is it that the world is falling apart as, as…
Never before?

An Induction

Little Tim asks, "Mother, mother,
What is that thing like no other?"
And Mother asks Tim to go near
So she can make him rid of his fear.
"That, Tim, is a tree. Isn't it beautiful?"
Tim nods but not understanding full,
"Mother, what is it used for?"
He asks further pushing his door.
"Well, it gives life to all."
"And doesn't it ever fall?"
"After a while it will."
This sad fact sent down a chill.
But even with his innocent face,
And untied shoelace,
Tim now knew that trees are for good
And plant more of them we should.
This is nice, you may say
But the day is centuries from today,
And why worry, you ask, about the date?
Because Tim is in a museum and it's too late.

The Shopper

There must be many like me on earth
Who are lost to reason and mirth,
And so we all eventually find the time
To lose our hefty minds for it is no crime.
When I am in the market I am not myself
My eyes just simply have to sail past every naked shelf,
Be it books, fruits, leather boots or underwear
When I see goods returned… in my heart there's a tear
For they must be weeping with failure to satisfy
Like a bird that is liberated but can't fly.
So I make it a point to not renounce things once bought
Or I'll be nothing more than a face in the lot,
In the batches that come merely to shop, I don't wish to belong,
I come here not because everything's right… but because nothing's wrong.
Often I hear children cry for new toys,
Sometimes I eavesdrop to hear girls discuss their boys,
And I see the bright lights that welcome all,
There are brisk voices out here and I hear them call.
And for me it's sheer joy to smell the smells,
It's remarkable the way every shopkeeper compels.
To measure my tranquil here there is no gauge
Every shop becomes a shrine and I become a sage.
When I have nothing to do this is where I'll be found,
Where there is nothing at all to which I can be bound.
If you think me a fool… think again,
Who has a beating heart and not love for a bargain?

Parting

One day it had to happen
But it happened too soon,
Our minds are now a sweaty summer,
But our eyes a wild monsoon.

In this abundant world
There are few we call friends,
Almighty has so many resources,
But only a few companions he sends.

I can only pray that
Forever pleasant are your days,
Life can be an extensive field,
Considering you find the rays.

Parting is an obnoxious ritual
But there is nothing we can do,
Before we were in the cosset of gardens
Now we face the dew.

All that I can prescribe is
Beware the worldly frauds.
For we are nothing but rolling dices
In the hands of cold gods.

August

What a fine class it is which
Burns to tell what it doesn't know,
Dives into arcane heights and brings alive a game,
Imagine in spans that it can tame.
I see you, oh versifier, trapped in your dark nights
Burned in honey and singing colored kites.
Dazed in collision with all that's thinkable,
You shine in your own preamble.
But what do you get by it all,
Wasps of poverty and the nightingale's call?
Or do you compose to alter destiny,
With the lyrics and rhymes of your mutiny?
Yet I pity you and encourage,
For I love your offense and the image.
With that scholarly crown,
You jot down every seen smile and unseen frown.
The gripping pen and the core profound,
You dance and make us dance in your own sound.
Your mind is ours and if not like, better,
For we think of our balances and not the emoted fretter.
Burn down, I pray, in your own insanity
Which is stranger than ours but not a vanity.

Survive and last in your strain,
For your August should not die in vain.
The Venetian blind you drape stings like a bee,
The humidity left behind, addictive as coffee.
Thoughts may melt but you prolong,
Your thumps are the music in our song.
Your defeat is the whitewash of Earth,
For a world without verse is like a joke without mirth.
Bear the estrange and rinse out the tar,
For life is merely a battle, but poetry a war.

An Ode to Cigarette

Just like a dressed bride of lack
Can't be told of a second thought,
So is a cigarette once out of the pack,
And she must be lit once bought.

Hers is a heart I set to fire,
And enjoy the very sight
'Cause only then can she fill my heart's desire,
And make my mind go light.

She fills me up till I'm really sated
Then I push the smoke out in lazy rings,
Against her effects many have debated,
But only a smoker knows the state she brings.

You can hide and you can run
And you can even quit her for good,
Her filter paler than the rays of the sun,
She could kill you, but do you think she really would?

Doctors, mothers, teachers alike
They all tell me to fight her temptation,
But I tell them all to take a hike,
Because whenever I light her, I'm on vacation.

The same people who drive trucks all day
Complain of my petty pollution,
I'm shoved into smoking rooms and kept from bay,
Because they think it's an apt solution.

Her package displays kind information:
That she is injurious to health,
But when I'm lonely in my bathroom or nation,
She's all I can call my wealth.

I Forgive Thee

"When they tugged me through the streets with a cold chain,
It certainly did not pain,
Humiliation never did occur to me,
I knew my sacrifice wasn't in vain.

When they threw stones at me as they would on a cur
Perhaps they were in a blur,
Pain never did occur to me,
My potency none of them could ever slur.

When they made me bear the tree like a mule
Their love was all I needed as a fuel,
Hate never did occur to me,
Though my father said I'd face it in the duel.

When they hung me on the wood and left me for days
I wasn't ablaze,
Death never did occur to me,
But the heavens were in a rage.

When I faced your being disloyal to me,
Failure was all I could see,
But thy deception never did occur to me,
Thus, go, Judas, for I forgive thee."

Goodbye

It's hard for me to wait for you, my love
See you in some other life. I
Hope you have a good time with
Your empty lovers.
It could be a lifetime before
I see you again, so don't look
In the mail for any postcards from me.
Years and years hence when you look
For me, remember,
I'll be the one
You never had.

Her Melody

Insane worlds trapped between,
Yet Physics argues the distance is ten yards,
I try to locate a lazy corner I've been
And instead find the verve of a thousand bards.

She plays the piano hush and unsaid
As I come home and loosen my tie,
Tunes like constables chase me in my head,
Till all the wayward men in me die.

Into her walls she invites me each evening
But forgets to send an invitation,
So I can only hide and hear her song,
And not even clap for fear of inflammation.

She plays a tune I've never heard
And I'm quite sure she hasn't as well,
But I can't retort to an unspoken word,
Not if it makes me forget I'm in hell.

Her window so close to mine
But her world farther than a tea-stall in Mysore,
Fingers cannot play something as divine,
Without interruptions from a murky core.

But then all that is celestial changes face
And emerges the darkness of a rainforest,
Where corrupting fruits find a place,
And talking snakes not too honest.

Temptation is no more a scarlet sample,
Things have changed since then,
Today a lady who plays the piano is ample,
For harmony alone can transform men.

Salesmen

They emerge suddenly on
Corners with pamphlets
For an unthought-of jeopardy, and so we
Are doomed.
For how can a simple man combat
Forces that could effortlessly
Sell a copy of the Bible to
The Man upstairs?

I'm afraid.

Pick up your phone and
You'll end up
Buying a purifying
Solution for a water pump or
An extra bulb for an
Emergency light that
You don't
Have.

I'm afraid.

I thought I was
Young but
Then I met a salesman, I
Thought I was old
But then
I met a
Salesman.

I'm afraid.

Danger

If hazards were in the crux
Of her hair,
This dream would be a terrible one indeed.
However, in my mind I'm the messiah
And shall allow no such
Peril on my subject,
Save a stray wolf like myself to lazily
Gaze.
Look at her as her feet ploy
And the absence
Of dreams make her stumble, which
As a matter of fact happens to be
What I hate about youth.
Only you and I can see her
So we have nothing to genuinely worry about.
The only precaution is patience
And I deem we are low on stock, for
When beauty strolls down the alleys
That's when we
Come out of our cages.
A simple whistle can gnaw at
Her temples till the most innocent
Thoughts evaporate.
Like a gypsy girl lost in the woods
She senses danger and quickens her pace,
I let her leave because I know
We'll meet again.

The Patient

I'm yet to wake up that day when I don't ever want to sleep,
I'm yet to be struck with despondency so hard that it makes me weep,
I'm yet to pick a road and consider walking it all the way,
I'm yet to saunter into the house of God and say that things are okay.
I'm yet to find a moment when I can promise my soul is wholly clean,
I'm yet to locate a place that doesn't take me back to places I've been.
I'm yet to lust for a substance that has filled all my heart's desire,
I'm yet to go to sea a day and truly want to return to the pier.
I'm yet to discover anger so cold that it could freeze my heart,
I'm yet to meet a person with whom I could readily part.
I'm yet to taste a dish that perfectly parachutes over my appetite,
I'm yet to find a fresh issue over which no one else has had a fight,
I'm yet to hear a song that whitewashes every shady memory lane,
I'm yet to see a sight pleasing enough to give my eyes pain,
I'm yet to arise to a position when I think I've had it all,
I'm yet to be of a complexion that alters my skin into a shawl,
I'm yet to grab a pen and write everything I've had in mind,
I'm yet to look back at history and wish I was left behind,
I'm yet to walk into a crowd and not feel alone,
I'm yet to feel glad for the thousand times I picked up my phone,
I'm yet to stare into nature's canvas and not feel inferior,
I'm yet to stand in darkness and not sense someone near,
I'm yet to explore a pair of eyes and unearth love as famished as mine,
But I can wait, I guess, because I have the time.

Role Models

They don't sit behind desks at universities,
Nevertheless their morals are as intense,
Indeed further.
Waifs and strays since childhood but
Never take it as a digestive excuse and continue
To gaze into the mists of time,
For a single trace of aid.
Once they mature,
Envy and lassitude don't crack their wits.
They swing on the vines of their past to be reminded
That future always has a trick up her sleeve,
Something we can never be au fait with
Despite extravagant hours with doctors and shrinks shrinking
This poor mind.
Never claimed by the labyrinth of triumph or the scandals of gloom,
These trifle issues,
Cut by the sharpness of direction.
They work day and night
Not troubled by overtimes and low remuneration,
They work incessantly.
Summers are heated by the keenness of awaiting rewards
Not rewards exactly—just simple bliss.
For when one plants the pip
He loves the thriving tree.

In winters they don't fly to beaches and sunny depots
But face their crafted fate
And labor.
Even if dictating snow-flakes freeze their craniums or
The sloshes of winter rain congeal their spines.
They continue to walk up and down life's huge hills,
With their heavy prizes and no unpaid bills.
Legion is the only religion and
All chattels are prey to all for one and all for
One.
If one steps on the other
The latter gets his head crushed,
But not rise to protest
Rather die.
Their eyes should have acres of proud twinkles,
Yet they don't wish their names found in golden words
Or in morning sermons.
They don't want to walk into the festivity of the future
Without an invitation card.
They mind their own affairs, even if kismet poisons.
And still labor.
There is only so much we can learn from ants.

Anonymous

Just another face in the crowd,
Just another voice that's not too loud.
Just another hand that you never shook,
Just another set of eyes in which you can look.
Just another foot that will take paths unsigned,
Just another life that death left behind.
Just another riddle to which you have no clue,
You are monotonous to me and I'm anonymous to you.

Exit

A spell of evening breezed through
A thousand sunsets crumbled,
And in the house across the dew
Mr. Becker lay troubled.

He was in the spirits, too
Gulping sweet nature wine
But perhaps his thoughts were too
Paralyzed by the passing time.

No partner, no heir in this ramble
So many unopened books in his life,
His book the only without a preamble,
Reason enough not to strife.

The man of sixty-eight got up,
Took a glance without amuse,
His soul now akin an overflowing cup,
He just couldn't refuse.

Where did he go? He just disappeared
Ah, there he is above the bed,
And just as I feared
He's hanging; he's dead.

The bitter medicine for this loneliness,
An exit from this world and an exit from this mess.

I Am Safe

Behind this cigarette my spirit is aflame
As I account all the tanks that surround,
I can no more be a clapping audience in this game,
I was born to humanity but to a country am bound.
Put a gun to my head and chances are I'll submit
Our leaders, fancy bullets and not fodder,
I lie at home guilty of a crime I didn't commit,
All because someone didn't want to share a border.
Children in lands I know nothing about
Wave their guns when they should be reading,
And activists here safely get bored and shout,
As long as they know they are not the ones bleeding.
Talks on tables are easy, Mr. President,
But it's another cup of tea once overseas,
You shake hands with other politicians with no lament,
But what of the men who beg for life on their knees?
You can raze a nation and build it again;
These are performances that I have seen before,
But every child that looks for his one-time home in vain,
Is a cub that will surely grow up to roar.
Breaking news, hostages, peace talks and seasoned bombs,
Beyond this there seems to be nothing more,
In seconds we could all be hushed under tombs,
So I go to bed remembering to latch the door.

Dirty Business

Richard is out of town and at last I'm free,
To make my decisions without his decree.
I stand here nervously in this infamous district,
For a man who, I hope, is not too strict.

And approaches me slyly does he,
Pulls out his asset and shows it to me.
All I can do in wonder is give it a stroke,
He says he wants me to have it before he finds a bloke.

A good tool in my hand I hold,
My husband's got one but not so bold.
This one looks slick and long-lasting,
And the soft texture makes good casting.

I want it fast but can't really rely,
On the dirty business and this unknown guy.
A thing as fresh as this is just what I need,
It looks kind of small but will satisfy my greed.

He wants me to show the money before we continue,
I hope he doesn't know that in this business I'm new.
A housewife of thirty-eight who of life is wary,
I will take it from anyone—Tom, Dick or Harry.

My husband warned me about such an affair,
But a deal like this is just too good to share.
So I'll give him the money without any guarantees or grounds,
And buy this Nokia 9110 for only sixty pounds.

I Ask You...

Columbian villas and blank cows,
Anxious mothers and gold watches,
What's my worth?
Crafty gatekeepers and flaunting mannequins,
Wooden dustbins and chatting stars,
What's my worth?
Neutral bodyguards and hopeless assets,
Honest chemicals and shifting fashions,
What's my worth?
Gigabyte computers and bought love,
Matching buttons and clichéd critics,
What's my worth?
Debating tanks and drained syringes,
Pungent ministers and calm graves,
What's my worth?

The Liar

I know it's wrong but I do it anyway
For my life has only rain, not a single sunny day.
I'm afraid they won't accept me if I told the facts
So I go along and form my own one-way pacts.
I don't have a fancy car and hence I lie
So every girl I meet does not pass me by,
I don't have a mansion unlike what I say
But if a room is fine, then drop by someday.
I tell the boys I have won all the fights
When really even girls can knock off my lights,
And I tell the women I have hotels in Sydney
But just last month I had to sell my kidney.
I tell my girl that I can't visit due to case studies
When I am really drinking a case at a buddy's,
And I tell this buddy that I can't pay
Because my girl's eye operation took everything away.
They have never found out, as I'm good
But when they will, hate me they truly would.
Because I'm the worst liar around, deep down in a mess,
I lie to the priests when I go to confess.
I belong to the kind who blames the car for delay
So pay attention to me, pay heed to what I say.

For we liars are quite a lot in number
We'd rather lie than in truth find slumber.
People will find out so I can't even die,
They'll know that my uncle is no Russian spy.
They know that a supermodel is not whom I date,
They'll know that my bicycle was the real reason I was late.
They'll know that my house has no swimming pool
In the backyard,
They'll know that I was a drunken menace and not a bard.
And if you feel sorry for me then extinguish that fire,
For I was only lying when I said I was a liar.

Distressed Woman

I make out that she is just fifty-seven and
Recall the great number of stories about her,
Though I forget the stories themselves.
I remember something about her glowing birth
Midst times of shade
And how it changed
The vicinity.
She loved to sculpt and paint and I've been fortunate
Enough to see some of her works. All was well until a stranger
Had her lured and plundered her
Simple spirit. The fault, I think, was
Partly hers for sporting gold jewels on
The dark night.
Her wedding was the most grand and
The whole world seemed to celebrate.
In dowry, I hear, she had to pay a tidy sum;
Depart with a dear sister,
But matrimony is a prize indeed and sacrifices are not hassles.
Now she's in a larger family and resides
In the apartment next to mine.

Her screams and wails keep me awake at night,
And a part of me thinks it's the fault of the stranger who
Once promised her the world and instead
Chained her in some dark dungeon where she couldn't sing,
Dance or paint.
I have seen her eyes and
They have illness manifested in them, an excuse
That her sons gladly use to not be the
Stick to a tired pile as such.
My father says that she was probably merrier with the stranger than
Her family, but I
Don't think so.
She may be distressed but she is a mother,
Her groans are temporary; I hope nothing further.
I think I should help, lend her a hand,
After all, she is India… my motherland.

Around the World

An Indian market flooded with spices,
Nepal, a shrine midst the rolling dices,
Luxurious Thai beaches could make you cry,
Especially along Chinese plateaus that are dry.

London is a fine city even if you have a heart,
Paris is the one that jolts me with its copious art,
In Italy true love is not very difficult to find,
But in Amsterdam the pursuit could leave you
Behind.

Anxiety in Mexico is understandable you'll agree,
Liberated Kenyan lions could make you climb a tree,
Antarctica is cool and I don't mean in fads,
Dublin, a town of mischievous lads.

And what can I say about the warm California sun,
Under which it is manual to carry an automatic gun,
Brazil is at ease with its coffee and football,
Afghanistan could really use a shopping mall.

Land of dawn at the rise of cheap calculators,
Moscow snared under its political alligators,
Australia is but a case of beer cases,
Germany no more has unfriendly bases.

I've been around the world though I never left my room,
I love my vogue of traveling though it means accurate doom,
A shame my frequent flying doesn't get me any points,
But who needs a silly discount when I have all these joints?

Much Simpler

Ages ago when the human
Mind was nothing but a seedy vegetable,
It awed the unknown.
A caveman would stare at the great ball
For hours together not knowing it's been hours together.
Rain was smelt and quickly worshiped.
More forceful than the mighty winds was
The fear alive in the ancient man.
Chivalry had not yet taken birth but unfortunately
Curiosity had, and it killed cats later
And minds first.
No more were elements stupidly adored,
We found gods.
What emerged was an empire never thought of,
A paradise where all would
Be equal and gas pumps serve
Cheeseburgers at midnight. Where one
Remote would operate any idiot box in the world similar
To how an idiot box operates
Any idiot in the world.

In this realm now nothing lies unknown and
No stones unturned. Storms whistle in windmills and
Rain plays in man's lap.
Solar energy makes fried rice in Chinese villages and Pluto
Can be seen for ten dollars in air-conditioned comfort.
Fire is an unwelcome guest who last visited
The roof of the world.
Yes, things have become simpler, much simpler and man
Fears nothing but
Himself.

Silly Dreams

At a park today
I saw some children play in their white,
Pure worlds. And
This silly heart did
Wish I had a son to gift baseball bats to.
As I crossed a road
I swear I spotted a car that should have
Been ours. For it was
Painted a blue too parallel to
Your eyes and my favorite cap.
I bumped into a house that
Said it wanted to
Be a home. And I promised to
Return knowing you
Would adore the white fences.
And then I came to surprise but
Surprise came to me. Your room smelt
Of cigarettes. You don't smoke, dear, but I'm sure
The new guy does.
I thought I had the key to Heaven only
To find that you had a
Spare.

Love of an Alcoholic

He didn't get me
No fancy ring that could
Parade up and down my finger,
But he loves me
And how.
This is one man that
Cupid assaults every day and
Yet only injures.
We are both loose and counterparts in
Thoughts and deeds.
Look at him as he opens my door, and
How he stares, Adam must have
Judged Eve like so.
No word of greeting; it's his manner
To reach out and pounce
At the object of his affection.
I hope I'm dressed for the occasion, albeit the
Only way I can make this relationship
Work is by letting him confiscate my top.
He looks through me as if
I'm an hour glass and hold the merit
Of his present.

Two hands slide around my back and
He lifts me higher and
Higher,
And all that I hold within is giddy.
His eyes tell me that I'm not
The first he's met tonight,
But I'm content to be the finish of
A long day of passion.
The bedroom is dark but here we can't see
Each other give in to
Each other.
Observe how calmly he gets his mouth
Near mine, and kisses me
Like a lost explorer kisses a new land.
He holds me over and continues to
Drain all I hold within, with his mouth
Still deep in mine.
Yes, yes
I think I'll definitely be the one he'll remember
Tomorrow as love, for I am
The last bottle of beer in his refrigerator.

London Girl

In a town where love is
Advertised in phone booths and acquaintances
Stop to gape at neon billboards,
You, too, exist.

In a town where a mobile queen is
Guarded by immobile guards and bridges
Shake hands,
You, too, exist.

In a town where every sketcher is
Looking for another face and time
Declared with cordial chimes,
You, too, exist.

In a town where the world is
Introduced to the world and jewels
Evermore shine on,
You, too, exist.

In a town where everyone is
Drinking to forget what they don't remember and life
Halts in many veins,
You, too, exist.

That's why I love this town.

Simple Solutions

The hammer of heat pounded my head
And I evaluated walking to lying in bed,
But a voice from within made measurements,
Of ways my destination could rub out my laments.

When a vacant hand finds no other as cold
It will gladly cherish anything that serves the purpose of hold,
Truth played in the backyard of my brain without a torch,
But she was there because fear had occupied the porch.

So I did keep moseying up the hill in faith
That once I reached the shrine there'd be no wait,
For in God we trust and I thought He would know for sure,
That my heart was in gutter and my salary even lower.

It was early in the morn and hence no crowd,
Divinity sits bored with no one around to be proud,
But I thought I could exploit the solitude,
By debating with heavens and not found rude.

This collateral notion became out of order
When I encountered a boy at the temple's border,
And what amused me was the way he was amused,
If joviality is a crime then he truly stood accused.

I walked up and asked him what he found so witty
For I rarely bump into joy for I live in the city.
"Today is the best day, sire, believe me when I say,
For I've solved everything and now there's no need to pray."

In his voice there lied no lies
And naked satisfaction danced in his eyes,
So I asked him to kindly explain,
What he meant by the statement inane.

He grabbed my hand and led me with some intent
Into God's house where no one else was present,
And then he pointed in a direction and said,
"You are in the house, sire, and the dweller is dead."

It was only when I followed his finger and saw
That I was shaken with an air so raw,
For lay before me the broken divine figure,
Stones all about now absent of any vigor.

"What have you done, you fool?!" I yelled.
"I simply killed God, the same that had me compelled."
"You've broken a statue, boy, nothing more!" I snapped.
"I thought it was here that all my problems cropped."

Some troubling thoughts knocked on my mind—
What would the many devotees like me come to find?
Would anger be the child of this juvenile mischief?
Or would they go further and sink in grief?

To answer myself I asked myself what I was feeling
And to my dismay found that I couldn't go on kneeling,
A stone was all I had worshiped all my life,
When it hadn't ended wars nor my strife.

I faced the boy and said in vain,
"Go home now, and don't do it again."
He started walking but left with his witty knack,
"A second time is uncalled for; dead men never come back."

It was a long way back home but now I was wiser
Despair will be for dessert if blind faith was the appetizer,
You may have punished the boy for his action uncouth,
But I'm a crazy man and I say holier is a phone booth.

Insipid Times

Another day in absence holding your hands
Behind the lines of a darker recall,
Clasping on is arduous because
Decisions made wrong can wind up in wind.
Effigies of civilization are commonly uncommon on
Fanatic planets, where all that can be recycled is
Greed and dust from under our closed doors.
Hungry as we are upon the table of time,
I cannot wait any longer for the morsels of peace.
Judging by the ingredients and spices we use
Knavery is all we'll have for dessert.
Lonely as reliability itself; now
Methinks it impossible to walk the emerald mile and
Not be hit with a single ailing stone.
Of where we go I shall leave to you, because
Part of me believes that once we answer the
Question there will be many more to
Resolve whether we like it or not.
Still I believe that time shall unleash a paradise.
Tomorrow we shall ponder over this hidden corner.
Uncovering a honeyed depot is a task
Very few can finish,
We've got nuclear bombs to tackle and maddening crowds
Xeroxed with religions, in addition some may say
You and I are
Zany.

Last Train on a First Platform

Zebra-print underwear is just one of the things
You make me encompass in my mood, and all
Xylems in my true theme have broken
With time.
Very, very, very
Useless is a heart as two-sided as
The one that governed me.
Sleeping by your side, I have advised
Racketing gods that their
Quests are exhausted, because
Pondering over you has become the real
Objective of my
Napping ambition.
Me on the last train to nowhere and
Leaving you is not my answer,
Knowing me, but
Just my question.
Illness of choices is a trick that
Hides in every road, and
Given that, you can be sure that when you'll
Forget me, I shall return.
Endings don't begin until hearts
Destroy what they impel, so I call for
Ceasefire before I walk,
Because by you I stand
Alone.

Poetic Confession

I wish I could write a line
That a lesser man could later quote,
But I only record the seen landmine,
And not the unseen merry boat.

I wish I could make you see just pastures
While you turn these pages on,
But I see pains and no raptures
In my heart-shaped box all shrubbery is gone.

I wish I could take you away from these times
And talk about just the past,
But history, too, is not innocent of crimes,
So our joyride wouldn't last.

I wish I could only note the things I adored
While I hold a pretty hand,
But this stuff could get people bored,
For not many have a magic wand.

I wish I could erase the savagery
And all the silly tit-for-tat,
But I only use them in my imagery,
Because lying is something I'm not good at.

When in Venice

Remember to forget the
Carnivorous shylocks,
But don't forget to remember the
Assorted boats on the docks.
Remember to forget the
Hidden faces behind the masks,
But don't forget to remember the
Artists merrily executing their tasks.
Remember to forget the
Gondola's expensive shock,
But don't forget to remember the
Only roads on which you can't walk.
Remember to forget the
Many lovers dazed under the sunshine,
But don't forget to remember the
Way her eyes danced to the tune of the wine.
Remember to forget that
The waters are below and you above,
But don't forget to remember that
This is the right place for love.

Lisa's Appointment

I walked inside as he lazed
And I was again where I'd been before,
With an unhesitant façade he gazed,
Lest he got me sore.

I had called him and he said
It was time we met again,
Under his arms he had me led,
And I knew it was time for pain.

He started by sliding on a rubber
For without it I wouldn't let him arrive in me,
He had told me he was a regular clubber,
And believe him I did in glee.

Soon as he found his way in
I thought I'd gone numb,
His movement inside produced a din,
But I chose to naively play dumb.

He was so deep inside
That I lost power of speech,
With his knowledge I had to abide,
Or be worthlessly sipped by the leech.

As I lay in that position
I wished I could be at some other place,
He was respectable in his execution,
But I wish he had broken the pace.

He pulled his tool out of me
And told me to spit if I wanted,
Swallowing wouldn't be too bad he said,
But I chose to not take it for granted.

He said everything was all right
Only I thought he was finished too soon,
He switched on the light,
And told me to come some other noon.

Then it was time for unmasking
He gave me another appointment on his list,
Sometimes I find myself asking,
Why do I love to visit my dentist?

To Raoul Duke

In convertibles or on feet,
The world moves at the same speed,
D'you know what I mean?

Drizzling Loyalty

Only the absent remain
With the village in the vicinity of doom,
There are cyclones of blithe and some of gloom,
All of it in the rain.

There have been a hundred nights for sleepers
This parish seems quite harmless,
And love does on the silent mess,
For its balm for the consumed seekers.

Misty—dusty, full of prickly stones
And the grass polyglots with the chronicles
The fields left by the farmers and their sickles,
At this the pasture is alive, it moans.

The lake is the very blast of life
Where the village children do swim,
Contained it has but never angers above brim,
It swallows and spits, not the knife.

There is a gulch in my very past
Grown have I to be dressed,
I am abject as ever but my village yet blessed,
Beyond me and life it will last.

It seems there are no such things
As a heart in the village sore,
Here they have contentment to the core,
And oh, what rapture it brings.

The mania that has survived for centuries
Is the simple life in the hamlets,
As the sun rises and it sets,
Arises a beauty and ends the furies.

Life is the butter of mornings
Pretty rusty are the sounds,
The faces have their own rounds,
Fantasy erases frowning.

In the village—the villager his own
For God is the dweller of pure mind,
Here tainted questions you will not find,
Devotion is full, and full is it shown.

My village—the lode of silence
My village—far from your violence,
Where the artless and the artists both reside,
Where cloudless is love and strangers can hide.

Cover Your Ears

I stood before a tank when the time came
I wiped millions and all without shame
I clenched my fists more firmly because I was black
I walked on my mind because I had no back
I embraced patience when wickedly placed behind bars
I was done with the Moon so I moved to Mars
I played the guitar till the guitar played me
I received three bullets for setting my country free
I had a dream so my brothers could rap
I live to walk from every mishap
I hid in caves and shook the order
I laid my life so I wouldn't have to share a border
I found time for a thousand goals
I made journeys between the poles
I shook hands to make the largest construction
I killed myself when fame was a disruption
I completed marathons with a broken foot
I have jumped from skies without a chute
I have come a long way yet my shoes never wore
I am Man and I have every right to snore.

The Good Guy

When to hate someone I find
I would drive a sharp knife in that blunt mind
Till the fool on my feet lands
I could kick his face and stamp his hands.
If a gun is around, even better for
I would place a bullet or two in
His worthless heart, with a
Smile.
If there is no heartbeat, I would
Stab it and stir the insides as if
I was making soup.
Tomato is red so definitely on our menu.
If any bullets remain, I'd empty them in
His head till nothing remains to be
Aimed at. And all that intelligence would
Flow quicker than ever.
A few blows don't hurt when
One is dead, so I
Would rain them on the rat.
Punching bags are costly.

Of the torso, what could I do? Maybe
Throw it somewhere where
Biology aficionados could revise. If I had
The time and the right skills, it
Would be nice to carve pieces for my
Chess board with his
Skull. Chess is, after all, a game of
The mind.
His soul, too, would weep and close eyes,
When he sees nothing of his body lies.
I would wash the blood and then cigarettes buy,
Unless I hate you… I'm a good guy.

Parallel Universe

Mirror, mirror, on the wall,
You are the only one who hears my call.
Be it night or day, evening or noon
You follow me everywhere and never leave too soon.
In you I can forget the lies in which I dwell
You always listen and never tell.
My secrets are safer in you than my friends
You help me look inside and make basic amends.
Ice may be suffice to end the world in days
But your glassy abyss is where our fires are ablaze.
In your cosmos I become a man of my word,
You give me proposals and not one of them absurd.
The man you reflect is the one man I can't hide
I've lied to lovers but to you have never lied.
I face only myself but you face many
The best consultant in town, yet, you don't charge a penny.
One day I may have to run from your candor aura,
For I'm a little box and you are Pandora.

A Dance with Malice

Hair akin the desires of
A thousand rascals snared
In dark cells for deeds unknown, and
She asks me for a dance.
Would I let opportunity knock, and
Not open the door?
I think not, and gladly
Kiss the offer.
Hear how the musicians favor us, much like
Rain gods blessing farmers in lands that
I have only heard of.
They toil to awake the cobras in women
And I think they have thrived.
For look how slyly her feet move as if
She wants to tell of her swinging talents but then
Settles for letting me find out.
And I have found darkness,
Nothing more
Nothing less.
For when a woman peeps into the windows of a man,
Fears awake and like parrots we await
An earthquake.
Already the skyscrapers in my heart are down,
And yet her song and my dirge see no end.
My love in my arms says she loves me
I agree, though,
I know she lies.

On Air

A thousand eyes watch me each day,
They watch me do each thing I do,
Watching me is what gets them pay,
But I'm just another face in the long queue.
Every time I enter a shop,
Move in their professional eye sockets,
And I can sense them dial for a cop,
Every time my hand departs into the pockets.
They must watch me eat instant noodles,
And discuss my pallid diet,
They supervise my walk between the oodles,
Just in case I start a riot.
They watch me read books in trains,
They watch me read books in a bus,
They watch me read the people aboard airplanes,
And wait for me to create a fuss.
My classroom is where I'm taught,
But even that isn't safe from stare,
They want me to behave in the lot,
And do nothing that I can dare.
I go to the hospital in pain,
But my disease follows here as well,
There're eyes watching me go insane,
When I edgily ring the beckoning bell.

They follow me into the shadows of nightclubs,
And watch the progress of my affection,
They see me down unnecessary pints at pubs,
And decide when they can make an intervention.
If I'm late for work or play,
I can't accelerate my car,
For they're watching the road night and day,
And so I won't get far.
Airports, libraries, offices and wombs:
There is not left a corner on earth for solitude,
We could kill ourselves and yet even in tombs,
Their eyes would want to verify our mood.
Privacy today is as extinct as the kiwi
And a simple stalker is jailed for observations remote,
The government stalks us all day with its CCTV
And yet is bestowed with our vote.

Patient Papers

A girl holed up in a warehouse and
A boy strolling free on pavements, both agree
That paper is the most
Tolerant of ears.
Paper is a white flag from
Both the sides and
I can create what pleases
Me. Killing a man is
Easier than killing time, so I
Let paper talk me
Out of slaughters and yearn
For a queen who stays at
A stone's throw.

Technological Forces

People to the left of me
And people to the right
But who has the time to talk free
When there's a mobile phone in sight?
I wish I could lend an ear from these slayers
But that's too much to ask,
With their hearing plugged deep into cd players
They are busy clearing the empty task.
No one to touch our tearing skins
But their touch screen palmtops work just fine,
Love letters and flowers end up in bins,
Now she prefers receiving e-mails of mine.
Pythagoras would have loved the wrist-watch calculators
And the logical video game,
There may live a genius in the hundred waiters,
So he would have to fight for his name.
A man sits alone in a subway,
There may be a GPS on the buttons of his suit,
Watchers may tell you where he sits today,
But not where he wishes to sit today, in sooth.
I see children placed beside
And grinning laptops sitting on mothers' laps,
My own eyes open wide
When I think how television wrecks naps.
Technology is the advancing trend
In this sober planet of ours,
Nobody wants to be your friend,
When they can talk via radio towers.

To the Catcher

Locked in our naive cages,
There is no place for us here,
Everyone is busy being themselves.

Now I've Seen Everything

I was there when the whole earth shook
Because of the innocuous lives that war took,
I witnessed silently a country's shame,
Knowing she would leap beyond tame.
History stands pillar to my sight
For what I saw was no delight,
I heard about rabbles being led into showers,
From which they never returned—calm under flowers.
I've seen a man being killed, before his son, by reason of being Jew,
There were far more and grisly vistas, these are but a few.
I thought it was over, but I was wrong
The second war came with a bigger gong,
Children once more cried blood and broke down,
The leaders did nothing—not even frown.
I'll remember the days we had, coping with our race,
Fighting for petty honor and elfin disgrace.
And how can I forget an August bloom
That flushed into nothing but doom?
There was a loud mushroom, masterfully spread
About this in the funny papers I had read.

People said it was now over but nay it was from far
Time breaks our spines and spits it in tar,
We become nothing but the stuff from what we evolve,
I seriously counted the days this planet would revolve.
As I had thought—these combats never stopped
On greed, knavery and power they propped,
The civil wars, the guns in schools and a smashed building,
It's the same story in our glacial hearts, yet no welding.
And I recall this walk I took by a park
When my mind finally found its mark,
All the patience that had held me tall,
Vanished when I saw some women play football.
That's when I knew I had seen enough
This revelation made me wildly cough,
I could hear God in a sorry tone say to me,
"I'm sorry, there's a limit to what a man can see!"

What Lies Amid

When written and named imagination,
But when spoken and called exaggeration,
Then what we have are lies.

When clandestine and tagged sin,
But when confessed nothing akin,
Then what we have are lies.

When told to yourself and called sadness,
When told to others and named madness,
Then what we have are lies.

When included in speeches for claps,
And included in conversations for slaps,
Then what we have are lies.

When said for rectitude and called white,
But when told for wrong and invites a bite,
Then what we have are lies.

When in own ear and called soliloquy,
But when to millions and called philosophy,
Then what we have are lies.

When sung in every heart and for free,
But when put on paper and called poetry,
Then what we have are lies.

The Killer

There are few things on Earth more
Pleasant than the look
Of depreciation on a face that doesn't belong to
Me.
And I'm a killer; you can say that,
And I'm a stone; I will say that.
But your relater is no stalker that
Watches people like a hawk would
Mice, and wait for
Them to be poised at the end of their wit.
Nor do I fire starving firepower to
Wash history
Text books with a trail.
I don't do that.
A man who poisons another is
Not a coward, he is
Poison himself.
I, too, want to be venom; I, too, want to be malice.
Granting deaths that will set slower than
A dozen sunsets is just the kind of
Thing that finds an exultant place in my diary.
Killing a few men is flawed; sanity demands
Quantity.

Explosives get the amount right but
Remember, I said something
About deaths slower than a thousand sunsets.
And so I use the most
Effective and simple weapon of mass destruction.
Something that leaves no fingerprints
And leaves no strands of hair that could
Bring a taciturn detective knocking
To my door. Yes, watch out, for I have
The perfect formula that
Warrants a dawdling and painful death to the masses;
I drive my car in the twentieth century.

What I Could Do with the Rest of My Life

I would like to sit down
At Leicester square with a
Bottle of beer in one hand, and
A slice of pizza in the other.
And wait.
And wait for a girl
Who would like to sit down
At Leicester square with a
Bottle of beer in one hand, and
A slice of pizza in the other.
And wait.

Tourist

These feet once
Took me to an address where love
Had been a resident.
With a camera in one hand and
No map in the other, I walk again
Looking for a similar abode.
It's hard to ask for directions when
I'm looking for a castle built
In my own air. Time and time again
Some lanes ring a
Bell, but memory is
Nothing but forecast in camouflage.
Don't mind me
If I knock on your door one day, for
I'm just a sightseer and you
Just may be the sight
I want to see.

To Yossarin

Your missions and my visions;
The world hasn't changed much, my friend.
I, too, will flee, someday.

Printed in the United Kingdom
by Lightning Source UK Ltd.
103613UKS00001B/116